THE CLYDESDALE HORSE

By Ellen Frazel

Consultant:
Dr. Emily Leuthner
DVM, MS, DACVIM
Country View Veterinary Service
Oregon, Wisc.

BELLWETHER MEDIA • MINNEAPOLIS, MN

Jump into the cockpit and take flight with Pilot Books. Your journey will take you on high-energy adventures as you learn about all that is wild, weird, fascinating, and fun!

This edition first published in 2012 by Bellwether Media, Inc.

No part of this publication may be reproduced in whole or in part without written permission of the publisher. For information regarding permission, write to Bellwether Media, Inc., Attention: Permissions Department, 5357 Penn Avenue South, Minneapolis, MN 55419.

Library of Congress Cataloging-in-Publication Data

Frazel, Ellen.
  The Clydesdale horse / by Ellen Frazel.
    p. cm. – (Pilot books. Horse breed roundup)
  Includes bibliographical references and index.
  Summary: "Engaging images accompany information about the Clydesdale Horse. The combination of high-interest subject matter and narrative text is intended for students in grades 3 through 7"–Provided by publisher.
  ISBN 978-1-60014-657-2 (hardcover : alk. paper)
  1. Clydesdale horse–Juvenile literature. I. Title.
SF293.C65F73 2012
636.1'5–dc22
                                    2011013802

Printed in the United States of America, North Mankato, MN.

080111   1187

CONTENTS

The Clydesdale Horse

The city streets are full of energy as people gather on the sidewalks to watch a parade. Everyone is enjoying the festive performers and colorful floats. A group of tall horses rounds the street corner and comes into view. Thick, white hair covers the bottom of their legs and reaches toward their hooves. The crowd recognizes the magnificent Clydesdale horses and cheers!

Clydesdales are famous for the **feather** at the bottom of their legs. Feather keeps them warm while they work outside during winter. Clydesdales have been helping farmers for hundreds of years. They are **draft horses**, which are sometimes called heavy horses. They pull carts, plow fields, and perform other tasks that require great strength. Clydesdales are very **hardy** workers.

A Plateful
Clydesdales are known for the size of their hooves. One of their horseshoes is about the size of a dinner plate!

Clydesdales are nicknamed "Gentle Giants" because they are large, friendly horses. Their towering bodies are muscular and graceful. Their **gait** is very energetic. They lift their hooves high into the air and step forward with confidence and power. Clydesdales can grow to be 18 **hands** tall. They can weigh between 1,600 and 2,400 pounds (730 and 1,090 kilograms). Despite their size, Clydesdales have a very calm **temperament**. They are gentle and make great companions.

Clydesdales have thick, heavy manes. Their coats are most often a reddish brown color called bay. They can also be black, gray, and other colors. Clydesdales have white markings on their bodies called **sabino patterning**. Almost all Clydesdales have white markings on their face. Most also have white on all four legs. People try to produce this characteristic when they breed Clydesdales. They like the flashy look of white legs as a Clydesdale clops down the street.

In Scotland and Beyond

Heavy horses were used in wars during the **Middle Ages** in Europe. They were strong enough to carry knights with heavy armor into battle. These horses were often referred to as "Great Horses." They were covered in up to 80 pounds (36 kilograms) of armor. The knights they carried wore about 100 pounds (45 kilograms) of armor. That was a lot of weight to carry!

A Strong Foundation

Lord Darney and Prince of Wales are considered the foundation horses of the Clydesdale breed. All Clydesdales are related to these two horses.

In the early 1800s, farmers in an area of Scotland called Clydesdale wanted heavy draft horses. They bred the large European warhorses with the small draft horses they used on their farms. This produced big horses with large hooves. The size of the hooves helped the horses walk on Scotland's soft soil. The horses hauled coal throughout Scotland. Their journeys took them to the large city of Glasgow. It was there that the name "Clydesdale" was first used at a horse breed show in 1826.

People in Scotland wanted to find the best horses for different kinds of work. Around 1837, farmers started bringing their best horses to shows all over the country. These shows determined which farmer had the strongest, healthiest horse. The winning farmer received a prize and was asked to bring his horse throughout the region to breed with other horses.

The Clydesdale breed spread throughout Scotland and into England. Soon, all draft horses in Scotland were Clydesdales. The Clydesdale Horse Society of Scotland was founded in 1877. Around that time, many Clydesdales were brought to the United States, Canada, Australia, and other countries. In 1879, the American Clydesdale Association was created. It was later renamed the Clydesdale Breeders of the U.S.A.

Big Relatives

A group called the Select Clydesdale Horse Society started in 1883. The group did not last long, but it added the traits of large British draft horses called Shires to the Clydesdale breed. Shires and Clydesdales look very similar today.

Between 1884 and 1945, more than 20,000 Clydesdales were brought to other countries from Scotland. They were used in World War I, but they became less popular after the war. Farmers began to use tractors and other farm equipment instead of draft horses. The number of Clydesdales continued to drop over the following years. In 1975, the breed was considered to be near **extinction**. There were fewer than 900 female Clydesdales in the United Kingdom.

The breed increased in numbers in the 1990s. By 2005, there were around 1,500 female Clydesdales in the United Kingdom. However, as of 2010, this majestic breed is again in danger of extinction. Only around 600 new Clydesdales are **registered** each year in the U.S.

The Horse Down Under

Between 1924 and 2008, over 25,000 Clydesdales were registered in Australia. People used them for many types of work. Clydesdales were nicknamed "the breed that built Australia."

Logging, Breed Shows, and Driving

Today, Clydesdales still haul heavy loads and help on farms. They are often used in the **logging industry**. Loggers cut down trees and use Clydesdales to haul them away. This is better for the environment than using machinery. Some farmers continue to use Clydesdales for **driving**. The horses pull plows and other farm equipment through fields.

People also exhibit Clydesdales at breed shows. They show them in the Scottish tradition of line and harness events. Drivers put their Clydesdales in harnesses and hitch them to carts or wagons. Horses are judged on their size, **conformation**, and other physical characteristics. They are also judged on their driving skills. They get points for their gait and how well they respond to their drivers. Some events feature teams of Clydesdales driving together!

Clydesdales charm crowds with their grace in **dressage** and their skill in jumping events. Horses and riders train hard to be successful in dressage competitions. Horses learn to respond to all of their riders' instructions. In competition, they perform different gaits and movements in front of judges. They even do pirouettes, which are full turns performed at a **canter**.

Clydesdales do well in both hunter and jumper shows because of their **agility** and calm temperament. Horses jump over obstacles in both events, but the shows are judged differently. Show hunters are scored for their manner and style of movement. Show jumpers are judged on their ability to jump over obstacles in a certain amount of time.

Horse Ballet

Dressage is nicknamed "Horse Ballet" because of the grace with which horses perform.

Famous Clydesdales

British Household Cavalry Clydesdales

In the late 1900s, Queen Elizabeth II of England saw a Clydesdale pulling a milk cart. She liked the horse so much that she put it into royal service. It hauled a 90-pound (40-kilogram) silver kettledrum for the British Household Cavalry band. Clydesdales still work in the British Household Cavalry today. A Clydesdale must be able to carry an officer and two heavy drums!

Grant's Farm Clydesdales

Grant's Farm in St. Louis, Missouri was the home of U.S. President Ulysses S. Grant. This farm is now famous for its many animals, including a group of Clydesdales. The Clydesdales on Grant's Farm all have bay coats with white markings on their faces and legs. Many people visit Grant's Farm to see these great examples of the Clydesdale breed.

People enjoy Clydesdales outside of breed shows and competitions. Parades are not complete without a group of Clydesdales high-stepping their way down the street. They carry important people on their backs or pull elegant carriages past celebrating crowds.

Clydesdales are also used for trail riding and **therapeutic riding**. They even pull wagons and carriages that people ride for fun. In some cities, people can pay for a carriage ride through a park or along the streets at night. Everyone watches as these gentle giants clop by, showing off their strength and majesty!

Glossary

agility—the ability to move the body quickly and with ease

canter—a controlled gait that is faster than a trot but slower than a gallop

conformation—the correctness of a horse's bone structure and body to the standard of its breed

draft horses—large, tall horses used for heavy physical labor

dressage—a specific kind of horse training; dressage horses perform movements like spins and turns at the command of their riders.

driving—using a horse to pull a wagon, cart, carriage, or other vehicle

extinction—when every member of a species or breed has died

feather—the hair at the bottom of a Clydesdale's legs

gait—the way in which a horse moves; walking, trotting, and cantering are examples of gaits.

hands—the units used to measure the height of a horse; one hand is equal to 4 inches (10.2 centimeters).

hardy—having the physical strength to endure harsh conditions

logging industry—the industry in which trees are cut down, hauled away, and made into products

Middle Ages—a period in Europe that lasted from the 400s to the 1400s

registered—made record of; owners register their horses with official breed organizations.

sabino patterning—white markings on a horse's face and body; sabino patterning is caused by the sabino gene.

temperament—personality or nature; the Clydesdale has a friendly, energetic temperament.

therapeutic riding—horseback riding for people with disabilities; therapeutic riding helps improve their balance, strength, and self-confidence.

To Learn More

At the Library

Dell, Pamela. *Clydesdales*. Chanhassen, Minn.: Child's World, 2007.

Murray, Julie. *Clydesdale Horses*. Edina, Minn.: ABDO Pub. Co., 2005.

Peterson, Cris. *Horsepower: The Wonder of Draft Horses*. Honesdale, Penn.: Boyds Mills Press, 1997.

On the Web

Learning more about Clydesdales is as easy as 1, 2, 3.

1. Go to www.factsurfer.com.

2. Enter "Clydesdales" into the search box.

3. Click the "Surf" button and you will see a list of related Web sites.

With factsurfer.com, finding more information is just a click away.

Index

The images in this book are reproduced through the courtesy of: Mark J. Barrett/KimballStock, front cover, pp. 4-5, 16-17; Bob Langrish/Animals Animals – Earth Scenes, p. 6; World Pictures/Photoshot, p. 8; Stephen Shaw, p. 9; Sarah K. Andrew, pp. 10-11; Paul McKinnon, p. 12; Findlay Rankin/Photolibrary, pp. 14-15; Mel Evans/AP Images, pp. 18-19; Ryan Lasek, pp. 20-21.